Generis
PUBLISHING

AF593368

Ethical Matters in Adult Education: Mezirow's and Aristotle's Theory

Thomaitsa G. Theodorakopoulou

Title: **Ethical Matters in Adult Education: Mezirow's and Aristotle's Theory**

ISBN: 979-8-89248-688-0

Author: Thomaitsa G. Theodorakopoulou

Cover image: www.pixabay.com

Publisher: Generis Publishing
Online orders: www.generis-publishing.com
Contact email: info@generis-publishing.com

ETHICAL MATTERS IN ADULT EDUCATION: MEZIROW'S AND ARISTOTLE'S THEORY

I dedicate this book to my parents.

Thomaitsa G. Theodorakopoulou

Contents

FIRST CHAPTER 9

1. Introduction 9

1.1 Adult Education 9

1.2. Ancient Greek Philosophy 10

1.3. Connections between adult education and Greek philosophy 12

1.4. Ethical principals in the literature of Adult Education 13

1.5. Ethical principles according to Lambrina Gioti 14

1.6. Ethical codes, according to Gilman 15

1.7. Ethical Principles of the Adult Educator, according to the writer 16

SECOND CHAPTER 19

Jack Mezirow 19

2.1. Jack Mezirow- Transformative Learning 19

THIRD CHAPTER 25

Aristotle 25

3.1. Who was Aristotle? 25

3.2. Aristoteles and ethics theory 25

3.3. Aristotle and education 26

3.4. Ethical theory of Aristotle 26

FOURTH CHAPTER 29

4. Parallel examination of the two thinkers 29

4.1. Critical reflection is joint for the two thinkers 29

4.2. Aporia and Disorienting Dilemma. Do they have the same meaning? 30

4.3. Dialogue is common for both thinkers 31

4.4. The meaning of experience for both thinkers 32

4.5. Eudaimonia or transformation? 32

FIFTH CHAPTER 37

About ethics and adult educators 37

5.1. Aristotle's virtue ethics inform adult educator ethics 38

5.2. Mezirow about ethics and adult educators 42

Conclusions 45

Bibliography....... 47

FIRST CHAPTER

1. Introduction

The subject of this monograph aims to deepen the specific approach and its presentation, consequently focusing on the ethical part of adult education. This monograph highlights elements related to Mezirow's and Aristotle's theories on the issue of ethics. Both Jack Mezirow and Aristotle have addressed ethical considerations related to adult education, albeit from different perspectives. It is crucial to highlight that adult educators play a significant role in learning, and their ethical considerations are paramount.

This monograph aims to map the areas where the theory of Transformative Learning, expressed by the modern thinker of Adult Education, Jack Mezirow, and the Aristotelian aretology converge and diverge. Relying on literature, the monograph argues that the two theories share considerable similarities, particularly their emphasis on critical reflection, experience, rational dialogue, and disorienting dilemmas and ethical matters of adult educators. However, they also must diverge their approaches to specific ethical considerations in adult education.

1.1. Adult Education

Adult education refers to providing learning opportunities and educational experiences to adults beyond their initial formal education. Many adults seek further education and skill development, and it is essential to remember that this journey is continuous. This can include enrolling in courses or workshops to enhance their knowledge and skills in specific areas. Adults often engage in professional development activities to improve their career prospects. This might involve attending seminars and conferences or pursuing advanced degrees or certifications. Adult education can also address basic literacy and numeracy skills for individuals who did not have the opportunity to acquire them during their earlier years. The concept of lifelong learning emphasizes that education is a continuous process, and adults should continue seeking knowledge and personal growth throughout their lives. Brookfield advocates that "Adult learning is the result of interaction between adults, in the context of which experiences are analyzed, skills and knowledge are developed, and activities are carried out. (Kokkos, 1998, Theodorakopoulou, 2017)

1.2. Ancient Greek Philosophy

Ancient Greek Philosophy refers to the intellectual tradition of philosophical thought that emerged in ancient Greece. It is often divided into several critical periods and schools of study, including:

- **Pre-Socratic Philosophy**

Early Greek philosophers, such as Thales, Heraclitus, and Parmenides, understood the fundamental nature of the universe and the elements that compose it. The most famous Presocratic Philosophers were the following.

Thalis of Miletus was considered the first philosopher who proposed that *Water* is the fundamental substance of the universe. Anaximander introduced the concept of the *Apeiron*, the infinite and indeterminate principle from which all things come. Anaximenes argued that *Air* was the primary substance of the universe. Heraclitus was known for his doctrine of flux and the unity of opposites. He believed that the world is created by *"fire,"* opposition, and war between opposites, to which he adds: "Opposites have a single direction - from opposites, the most beautiful harmony is born." (Wikipedia, n.d.)

Parmenides has emphasized the unchanging, eternal nature of reality. Parmenides is best known for his idea that "being" is singular, unchanging, and eternal. In his poem, often referred to as *On Nature*, he argues that **"what is" (being)** is, and **"what is not" (non-being)** cannot exist. This leads to the conclusion that change, multiplicity, and motion are illusions. According to Parmenides, reality must be one, indivisible, and static. Pythagoras explored the relationship between numbers, mathematics, and the structure of the cosmos. Empedocles proposed the theory of four elements (earth, air, fire, and water) and the forces of love and strife. Anaxagoras introduced the idea of *nous* (mind) as the cosmic force.

- **Socratic philosophy**

Socrates **(469–399)**, a central figure in Greek philosophy, focused on ethical questions. Socrates, the father of Western philosophy, believed education had immense potential to nurture and refine individuals. He believed knowledge was a collective inheritance of humanity and that the pursuit of wisdom and virtue should be inseparable (Tarek, 2023). **Socrates** is one of the most influential figures in adult education, primarily through his **Socratic Method**, which involves asking probing questions to stimulate critical thinking and self-examination. Rather than simply imparting knowledge, Socrates guided learners to uncover truths through dialogue and questioning. This method is crucial in adult education, where learners are often encouraged to question assumptions, reflect on their beliefs, and critically analyze their experiences and knowledge. Adult learners, who bring a wealth of personal and professional experiences, can significantly benefit from this approach, as it promotes active engagement and the development of deeper understanding. Socrates instilled a desire for virtue in his associates, hoping they could attain nobility and moral goodness through self-care and self-improvement. He pioneered an "oral culture" in education, focusing on dialogue and questioning to elucidate fundamental concepts. His innovative pedagogy has shaped how we engage with knowledge and moral principles today (Tarek, 2023).

He believed in the value of critical thinking and the pursuit of knowledge through dialectical questioning in the Athens Agora with adults and showed great interest in young people. Socrates (470-399 BC), using the method of dialogue and the obstetric method, formed questions and answers, formulated the midwifery pedagogical method, and set a new dimension in the concept of education and lifelong learning. He mainly discussed and established that the action does not end at a certain age, but spiritual practice occurs throughout life.

- **Platonic Philosophy**

Plato, a student of Socrates, founded the Academy in Athens and developed philosophical ideas about the nature of reality, justice, and ideal forms. Plato dedicated his life to upholding Socrates' teachings. The Academy was pivotal in European education, welcoming female students and offering a comprehensive mathematics, astronomy, and geometry curriculum. Plato's educational philosophy emphasized imagination as a pedagogical tool, fostering analytical skills and creative thinking. His innovative use of imaginary scenarios, a precursor to contemporary case studies, enriched the educational experience and laid the foundation for subsequent pedagogical methods. His legacy continues to influence educational philosophy and practice. (Tarek, 2023). According to Plato, education, through observation, dialogue, and research, aims to research truth and man's spiritual liberation (Sepitanos, χ.χ.). The concept of lifelong learning exists in a seminal stage both in Plato's "Nomoi", where there is a discussion about the obligation of every citizen to be constantly active and to actively participate in the organization of the state, as well as in the **Platonic "Politeia"**, where is presented the lifelong education of philosophers contribution of education liberating the people from ignorance and turning their souls to the sun of truth, the Idea, which is the highest good for Plato (Lesky, 1972).

- **Aristotle's Philosophy**

Aristotle, a student of Plato, contributed significantly to philosophy, ethics, metaphysics, and the natural sciences. His works laid the foundation for many areas of Western philosophy. We will refer extensively to this great philosopher later.

Aristotle's concept of developing *virtue* through habit and practice resonates with modern adult education in leadership training, ethics courses, and personal development programs, where learning is directed toward improving character and ethical decision-making.

Both Plato and Aristotle regarded education as intrinsically tied to ethics and cultivating virtue. For adults, education was about acquiring technical skills or knowledge and becoming better and more ethical individuals. Plato's Academy and Aristotle's Lyceum were learning centers where philosophy and moral development were emphasized alongside other subjects. These ancient schools treated education as a means of developing the whole person, an idea central to contemporary theories of adult education, especially those that emphasize transformative learning and personal growth.

1.3. Connections between adult education and Greek philosophy

Adult education and Greek philosophy, two distinct yet interconnected topics, have significantly shaped human thought and society. The intersection of these two fields is not just profoundly significant but also offers a fascinating journey into the roots of adult learning today—such as self-reflection, lifelong learning, and the pursuit of wisdom. The emphasis of ancient Greek philosophers on education as a process of self-development, intellectual growth, and moral improvement resonates with modern concepts of adult education, providing a rich and enlightening area for exploration.

There are several connections between adult education and Greek philosophy. In ancient Greece, philosophical education was a central aspect of intellectual development. Philosophers like Socrates, Plato, and Aristotle often engaged in dialogues and discussions with students, emphasizing the importance of critical thinking and the pursuit of wisdom.

Greek philosophy, particularly the teachings of Socrates, Plato, Aristotle, and their successors, emphasized moral and ethical development, a fundamental aspect of adult education aimed at personal growth and character development. Greek philosophy had a profound and enduring impact on Western thought and education. Many contemporary educational practices and ideas have roots in ancient Greek philosophical traditions.

The idea of lifelong learning in adult education aligns with the philosophical tradition of seeking wisdom and knowledge throughout life. While adult education and Greek philosophy are distinct fields, they share common themes of lifelong learning, such as critical thinking, personal development, and ethics. The legacy of Greek philosophy continues to influence educational philosophies and practices, emphasizing the enduring connection between these two areas of human endeavor.

1.4. Ethical principals in the literature of Adult Education

«Discussion of the ethics of practice is a relatively recent phenomenon in adult education. Most practice ethics literature was published in the past 20 years» (Gordon, 2001). Freire states, «Education should raise the students' awareness so that they become subjects, rather than objects, of the world. This is done by teaching students to think democratically and to continually question and make meaning from everything they learn» (Fortaliza, 2007). Instead of trying to institutionalize adult education with a professional code of ethics, practitioners would be better absorbed in developing their values and understanding their work's historical and philosophical foundations. It is essential for participants and practitioners alike in adult education to recognize that choices are to be made. Experience and sensitivity in making such choices—not politically-inspired, standardized, professional codes of ethics—will lead to a high standard of moral conduct in adult education. There is no need to develop a professional code of ethics. (Carlson, 1988, pp. 174-175)

Ethics in adult education is a crucial aspect that governs the field's behavior, relationships, and principles. Ethical considerations are essential to create a safe, respectful, and effective learning environment for adult learners. In adult education, there is a significant divergence between the standard roles and the functions of educators (Gioti, 2010). According to the writer, some vital ethical principles in adult education must exist.

1.5. Ethical principles according to Lambrina Gioti

Empowering Adult Learners: Respecting the autonomy of adult learners is crucial. It empowers them to make informed decisions about their education, including choosing their learning goals and methods whenever possible.

Inclusivity and Diversity: Adult education should be inclusive and respect the diversity of learners, including their cultural, linguistic, and individual differences. Instructors should foster an environment that values and celebrates this diversity.

Building Trust through confidentiality: Maintaining the confidentiality of sensitive information shared by adult learners is a cornerstone of trust and respect in adult education. This includes keeping personal and academic records confidential and not sharing personal details without consent.

Informed Consent: Adult learners should be provided with all necessary information about their educational program, including costs, expectations, and potential outcomes. Informed consent ensures that learners make decisions with full knowledge.

Fair and Equal Treatment: All adult learners should be treated fairly and equally, regardless of their background, identity, or circumstances. Discrimination, bias, and favoritism should be actively avoided.

Academic Integrity: Instructors should promote and uphold academic integrity by discouraging plagiarism, cheating, and other forms of academic dishonesty. Learners should understand the importance of original work and proper citation.

Effective Communication: Instructors should maintain open and transparent communication with adult learners. They should be accessible for questions, concerns, and feedback and provide timely responses.

Safety and Well-being: Adult learners' safety and well-being should be top priorities. Adult educators should be aware of potential risks and take steps to create a safe learning environment.

Professionalism: Adult educators should exhibit professionalism in their interactions with adult learners, colleagues, and the broader community. This includes dressing appropriately, being punctual, and maintaining a respectful demeanor.

Continuous Improvement: Instructors should engage in ongoing professional development to stay current with best practices in adult education. They should also be open to feedback from learners and colleagues to improve their teaching methods continually.

Social Responsibility: Adult education providers should recognize their societal role and strive to contribute positively to their communities. This may involve offering programs that address societal needs and challenges.

1.6. Ethical codes, according to Gilman

Gilman (2005) also proposed several primary purposes of ethical codes for public administration as a sphere related to adult education. Codes of ethics make it more likely that people will act in particular ways. They achieve this by emphasizing the nature of their needs and, in part, the consequences of infractions.

• Strong standards of ethics can direct participants' actions toward doing the right thing. Being ethical ought to become second nature. Trainees can compare their activities to expected norms by using codes.

• Systems of ethics do not confer public moral immunity and individual moral autonomy. Servant from the duty to make sense. At most, codes of ethics offer a strong argument for acting in a particular manner.

• Codes of ethics can serve as a declaration for professionals by expressing the public's concerns. Ethical considerations in adult education are essential for building trust, fostering a positive learning environment, and ensuring adult learners receive a high-quality and respectful educational experience. Adhering to these principles helps create a sense of dignity, fairness, and trust among all participants in the educational process.

Understanding fundamental concepts that an adult educator should adhere to gives trainees a greater sense of security and the opportunity to use these guidelines. A code of conduct fosters educator professionalism and fosters public trust in educators. Codes can help people become more sensitive to ethical issues and make decisions in challenging circumstances. According to Kadlubeková (2016) moral values are "moral standards of behavior that are typically applicable and relevant to all antagonists. They should be honored, and adherence to them should be demonstrated in andrologists' real-life behavior and actions. Moreover, it also describes ethical principles derived from comparing the adult education industry's current sectoral ethical norms. All these principles are equally essential and presented here in a random order. Some codes contain several sanctions.

According to Malah Josef (2020), their nature and impact on the educator can be put into the following groups:

- Expulsion from the association/revocation of the membership.
- Suspension of the membership in the association.
- Warning or convicting members for their behavior.
- Loss/revocation of the certification issued by the association.
- Dealing with complaints with the option of using disciplinary proceedings.
- Dealing with complaints by using applicable legal norms and common sense.
- Using labor and legal norms.
- Prohibiting the use of the organization logo.
- Self-assessment using a tools list of professional standards.
- Withdrawing advertisements.
- Corrective correspondence with clients.
- Withdrawing literature, materials, and programs disrespecting code standard.

1.7. Ethical Principles of the Adult Educator, according to the writer

The role of an adult educator involves unique ethical responsibilities, as they often work with a diverse group of learners who bring a wide range of experiences, perspectives, and needs to the classroom.

Some fundamental ethical principles that are essential for adult educators are the following:

- **Respect for Learners**

The first and most important principle for adult educators is respecting adult learners, who are typically independent and self-directed. Respecting their autonomy means supporting their goals, decisions, and perspectives. Adult learners come from diverse cultural, socio-economic, and educational experiences. An ethical educator fosters an inclusive environment that values these differences. Protecting learners' privacy, whether in sensitive discussions or personal information, is crucial in maintaining trust.

- **Commitment to Professional Integrity**

Adult educators should present current, accurate, and relevant information to learners' goals. Staying current in subject matter and teaching practices is an ethical obligation to provide the best learning experience.

- **Promoting Critical Thinking**

An ethical educator supports critical thinking and encourages learners to question, explore, and analyze rather than passively accept information. Educators encourage their students to embrace lifelong learning by committing to continuous learning. Adult education often intersects with personal development. Ethical educators help students set and achieve professional and personal goals that improve their lives.

- **Set Clear Expectations**

Adult learners benefit from knowing what is expected of them and what they can expect from their educators. Clear communication of objectives, assessments, and rules is essential. When mistakes or misunderstandings happen, whether in assessment, communication, or content delivery, ethical educators own these errors and work to correct them promptly.

- **Avoiding Exploitation and Conflicts of Interest**

Maintaining professional boundaries with learners is essential, as dual relationships can compromise fairness. Adult educators are responsible for avoiding exploiting the power dynamics inherent in the educator-learner relationship. This includes not using learners for personal gain or taking advantage of their vulnerability. If any conflicts of interest arise, disclosing them transparently to all relevant parties is ethical.

- **Being authentic**

Authenticity is crucial for adult educators. Being authentic means educators are genuine, transparent, and true to their values, creating a trusting and open learning environment. For adult learners, who often come with varied life experiences and a strong sense of individuality, an authentic educator fosters a sense of respect and connection that enhances learning outcomes. Authentic educators stick to their values and demonstrate integrity in their teaching, whether it is through their commitment to fairness, openness, or dedication to student success. Authenticity requires educators to be consistent in their actions and words. Learners appreciate transparency in grading, expectations, and policies and are more likely to respect a transparent and fair educator. The authentic adult educator does not impose his views, does not manipulate, and does not deliberately lead his students in his way of thinking. He opens the horizons and allows his trainees to follow him effortlessly.

By upholding these ethical principles, adult educators foster a learning environment that respects and empowers their students, supporting their educational and personal growth.

SECOND CHAPTER

Jack Mezirow

2.1. Jack Mezirow- Transformative Learning

Jack Mezirow is a principal thinker in adult education who developed his categorization of Transformative Learning (TL) in the late 1970s and early 1980s (Kapur, 2006). Mezirow (1995) regards the primary goal of adult education as fostering transformative learning. Jack Mezirow popularized the idea of transformative learning in 1978, which was essential.

His theory lies in the hierarchy of theories concerning adult learning. The transformative learning theory is part of a broader range of constructivist theories, which heavily emphasize the independent learning of a single subject. A fundamental principle of the idea is that students' interpretations of their construction of meaning are significantly influenced by their experiences. Mezirow (1991) posits that transformative learning aims to help learners move from a simple awareness of their experiences to an understanding of the conditions of their experiences and, beyond that, to explain why they experience as they are and to action based on these insights. Three interrelated components are central to fostering transformative learning: the centrality of experience, critical reflection, and rational discourse. Experience is the starting point for transformative learning, as it is socially constructed and can be deconstructed and acted upon. Critical reflection is the distinguishing characteristic of adult learning, questioning the integrity of assumptions and beliefs based on prior experience. Rational discourse is the necessary medium through which transformation is promoted and developed. Mezirow believes that fostering transformative learning involves the most significant learning in adulthood, communicative learning, which involves critically identifying problematic ideas, values, beliefs, and feelings, examining their assumptions, testing their justification through rational discourse, and making decisions based on the resulting consensus (Taylor, 2000).

The hypothesis includes two categories of learning: communicative learning and instrumental learning. These categories focus primarily on problem-solving and how students express their wants, needs, emotions, and sentiments to one another. Individual meaning schemes or meaning perspectives impact how experiences are interpreted as "constellations" (Karavakou, 2018).

Mezirow (1978, 1991) developed the emancipatory ideas of Jürgen Habermas. He promoted the idea of "perspective transformation," which is the process of personal development through a change in how one views the world and oneself. He felt that an unexpected realization of "the basic structure of cultural and psychological presumptions that have constrained or warped one's perception of themselves and their relationships provided a means of changing one's perspective (Mezirow, 1991, p. 7). Mezirow argued that highly charged emotional experiences were a rich source of transformative education. Moreover, he acknowledged that educators offered, if not essential, then substantial assistance with the educational process. Even though educational travel does not symbolize a "life crisis," it has great potential to deliver emotionally intense learning opportunities rich in values (Pitman et al., 2011). Moreover, this action helps us to comprehend the right to exercise personal judgment as the ability of an individual to remove himself from their specific experiences, the social circumstances, and a particular social system of what is good or wrong and for a thoughtful relationship with it.

We view this act of "stepping back" as having great significance for realizing one's tra its, limitations, and purposes, as well as for accepting full responsibility for one's acts and, ultimately, for reconsidering one's position regarding what one believes to be good or right.

This “stepping back” had no particular significance in the Aristotelian framework, as no cognitive or valuational disorientation was prevalent in that era's culture.

Most of the time, TL is how people change their manners, interpret their experiences, and interact with the world. If an individual holds opposing viewpoints about something in the outside world, he becomes aware of it; if an individual determines alternatives available and brings changes in his perspectives of observing things, that means that he has brought **transformation** in some area of the surroundings, environment, or the world. (Karavakou, 2018)

Mezirow claimed that a sudden insight into 'the very structure of cultural and psychological assumptions which has limited or distorted one's understanding of self and one's relationships' was a certain way that leads to perspective transformation (Mezirow, 1991, p. 7).

Mezirow (1991) states that promoting transformative learning attempts to help participants move from a basic understanding of what they are experiencing to an understanding of the conditions that underlie their experiences or how they process analysis of seeing, thinking, assessing, feeling, and acting and also to understand the reasons behind their opinions on people behave and choose what to do depending on these insights (p. 197).

Three fundamental and related steps are involved in the nurturing process: application, evaluation, and reasonable dialogue. The student's experience is both the basis and the educational resource for transformational learning (Mezirow, 1995). Understanding is recognized as socially constructed, enabling both application and disassembly. Experience is the fundamental basis for critical thinking (Taylor, 2000).

According to the theory of Transformative Learning", an adult learner reflects and reflects critically on already accepted concepts, re-evaluates the previous assumptions on which beliefs are based, and takes action based on the insightful thinking that results from the transformed view as a consequence of his reevaluations (Mezirow, 1990). TL is how people change their manners; they interpret their experiences and interactions with the world. If an individual holds opposing viewpoints about something in the outside world, he becomes aware of it; if an individual determines alternatives available and changes his perspectives of observing things, that means that he has brought **transformation** in some area of the surroundings, environment, or the world. This theory owes Jack Mezirow characteristics such as "conception, name, basic concepts, basic formulation, and its development until the phase of maturity" (Lintzeris, 2010: 96), while St. Brookfield extended it by clarifying Mezirow's often abstruse reasoning (Kokkos, 2010).

Mezirow (1991) sees the goal of fostering transformative learning as helping learners move from a simple awareness of their experiences to an awareness of the conditions for their experiences (how they are perceiving, thinking, judging, feeling, acting—a reflection on process) and beyond this to an awareness of the reasons why they experience as they do and to action based upon these insights (p. 197) (όπως αναφ. στο Taylor, 2000).

Jack Mezirow was a prominent adult education theorist known for his work on transformative learning theory. He developed this theory to understand how adults learn and change their perspectives and beliefs as they mature and encounter new experiences. As conceptualized by Mezirow, transformative learning is a perspective that focuses on how adults can fundamentally change their beliefs, attitudes, and ways of thinking through a reflective and critical process. Mezirow's theory of transformative learning suggests that adults can experience profound changes in their thinking and perspectives through critical reflection on their experiences. Mezirow's work has significantly influenced adult education, and it continues to be relevant in understanding the process of adult learning.

Some key points about Mezirow's ideas on adult education include:

This transformation often involves shifting fundamental assumptions, beliefs, and values. Mezirow's work emphasizes the following key points:

1. Disorienting Dilemmas: Transformative learning often begins with a disorienting dilemma, a situation or experience that challenges an individual's beliefs and assumptions. Mezirow proposed that transformative learning often begins with the experience of a disorienting dilemma—a situation or event that challenges one's existing beliefs and causes discomfort or confusion. This disorientation can lead to critical reflection and, ultimately, transformation. This can create a sense of discomfort or cognitive dissonance.

2. Critical Reflection: Adult learners engage in critical reflection to make sense of the disorienting dilemma. Mezirow believed that critical reflection is a key component of transformative learning. Adults engage in self-examination, question their beliefs, and evaluate the validity of their assumptions in light of new experiences. They examine their existing beliefs, question them, and consider alternative perspectives.

3. Perspective Transformation: Mezirow emphasized perspective transformation as a central concept in his theory. Perspective transformation involves recognizing and challenging one's beliefs and assumptions, leading to a new, more inclusive perspective.

4. Through this process of reflection, adult learners may experience a shift in their perspective or worldview. They develop new, more inclusive, and more accurate world understandings.

5. Action and Change: Transformative learning is not just about changing one's thinking; it also involves changes in behavior and actions. Adult learners may take concrete steps to align their new perspectives with their actions and decisions. Mezirow recognized that transformative learning is not just a cognitive process but also an emotional one. Adults may experience a range of emotions during the process of transformative learning, including anxiety, uncertainty, and, ultimately, a sense of liberation and personal growth.

6. Learning Communities: Mezirow encouraged the development of learning communities or support groups where adults can share their experiences, engage in dialogue, and collectively explore their beliefs and values.

Mezirow's work has influenced adult education practices and encouraged educators to create learning environments that support transformative learning experiences. He emphasized the importance of critical reflection, open dialogue, and the creation of safe spaces for adult learners to explore and challenge their existing beliefs.

Overall, Mezirow's ideas on transformative learning have profoundly impacted adult education, helping educators better understand how adults learn, grow, and change throughout their lives.

THIRD CHAPTER

Aristotle

3.1. Who was Aristotle?

Aristotle was an ancient Greek philosopher and scientist born in Stagira, Halkidiki, Greece. At 17, he entered Plato's academy in Athens, where he remained until age 37. Philosopher, leading educator, and, undoubtedly, the most systematic and organized mind of antiquity. He was destined to pass on his bright spirit to his pupil Alexander the Great. He would establish his school, the famous Aristotelian Lyceum of Athens, where he would pass into immortality both for his teaching work and - above all - for the incredibly compositional ability of his mind.

The philosopher found that virtue is optional and freely chosen by man. The task of the Aristotelian orator is the individual who does not act morally and fails to understand and interpret the principles of the practices that govern social life. Any action that does not contribute positively to the social whole ceases to exist. Therefore, the role of adult educator becomes essential in guiding the community as a whole. Only with their help will the community's well-being go as a whole. The young person must learn what is appropriate to the free man and what does not stand in the way of acquiring virtue. In this context, the role of education and lifelong learning is decisive. These liberate the fields of practice and make wisdom a constituent of primary importance.

3.2. Aristoteles and ethics theory

Aristotle was the first to deal with ethical problems systematically. He is the founder of Ethics as a philosophical science. Aristotle examines the ethical problem in ETHICAL NICOMACHEIA. Morality is the virtue of every human being. Virtues include diligence, rhythm, courage, sincerity, endurance, patience, perseverance, wisdom, discretion, discernment, discrepancy or discreetness, prudence, generosity, and others. Virtues are necessary for our lives because they lead us to our best selves and our best life and protect us from the impasse, such as great passions, depression, anger, addictions, fears, madness, etc. **The intellectual virtues are Wisdom, wisdom, and discretion (Filosofikilithos. n.d.).** Intellectual virtue primarily presupposes teaching for this and requires some time to acquire the individual's experience gradually. On the contrary, moral virtue presupposes the individual's will to become addicted gradually. In a particular way of behavior; moral virtues are actions of will (Γκότσης, 2018). "It is not introduced from outside into the soul of man by knowledge or teaching the moral rule but requires the exercise of the horse part of the soul according to the demands of the rational part repeatedly (Γκότσης, 2018).

Aristotle's ethics are **rationalist ethics.** The source of ethics is **rational reason**. He discovers and determines the appropriate ethics. Emotion, conscience, or divine law are not appropriate in assessing morality.

3.3. Aristotle and education

The essential prerequisites for education, according to Aristotle, are nature, habit and logic. The term "nature" means inheritance. All these characteristics of the person are regarded as acquired from his parents. The concept of habit means the exercise and the practices that people will do during their life and, in the sense of the word, understand the teaching that the individual receives, which at one point and then is the state's primary concern (Palazi, 2018).

As his teacher Plato had done, Aristotle emphasized and re-emphasized the great importance of education for the individual's private and public lives. All this is because Aristotle believed that with education and education addicts, the individual learns a specific behavior and is used to obtain virtue.

The sooner education begins, the more hope will be. It is proven to be effective and fruitful (Γκότσης, 2018).

3.4. Ethical theory of Aristotle

Aristotle conceives ethical theory as a field distinct from the theoretical sciences. We study ethics to improve our lives; therefore, his principal concern is the nature of human well-being. Aristotle follows Socrates and Plato in considering virtues central to a well-lived life. Aristotle classifies human virtues into two categories: intellectual virtues, which are connected with the rational part of the soul. Moral virtues are associated with the third part of the soul, which participates in both the soul's logical and moral parts and the reasoning part. Moral virtues are generosity and wisdom. Intellectual virtue comes and grows with theoretical teaching, which requires experience (reflection) and time. Moral virtues grow with habits. That is why their name—ethos—differs slightly from the custom ethos.

According to Smith, in his Ethics, Aristotle indicates the ways that man regulates his behavior through different nations, such as "the freedom, the majesty, the generosity, and even the joyfulness and the well-being, qualities, which this merciful philosopher judged values to be included in the list of virtues" (Triantafillidou, 2018).

In transparent ways, Aristotle's ethical philosophy leads to happiness. Happiness comes after strengthening the virtues, as a good habit, and meeting external needs because our body needs to be healthy and receive the care it needs. Man cannot seek happiness in fun. The happiest life is the one that is made according to logic (Γκότσης, 2018).

According to Aristotle, ethics did not aim at knowledge but character (Δραγώνα, 2015). Ethics had a deeper purpose than the simple transmission of knowledge. It is intended to sculpt and mold people's character based on pure virtues and values.

FOURTH CHAPTER

4. Parallel examination of the two thinkers

Parallel examination of the two thinkers, who belong to separate periods and different milieus, is related to their shared proposition concerning the dialogue with ourselves (Mantzanaris, 2018). Both thinkers state that ethical responsibility and learner respect are critical. They also share a concern for personal development and critical reflection. Furthermore, both thinkers underline the importance of experience, distinguishing adults from non-adults. Moreover critical reflection and disorienting dilemma or aporia regarded essential for both philosophers. Dialogue is another essential issue that concerns the two men and eudaimonia or transformation.

4.1. Critical reflection is joint for the two thinkers

Critical reflection involves thinking about teaching and learning by attending to cues within the teacher's tolerance limit. It is about making appropriate decisions about adapting teaching to best achieve teaching and learning objectives (Rotidi, 2015).

Both thinkers emphasize the rectum reason. Mezirow names it "critical contemplation' and "critical self-reflection," while Aristotle identifies it as the intellectual virtue of "phronesis".

Mezirow claims that adult trainees carry out critical reflection and reflective dialogue, while Aristotle says that wisdom, like all virtues, is praised by the social whole, the city. This is one difference between the two thinkers. Mezirow expresses that critical reflection, based on its purpose, is distinguished into: α) aimed at learning to solve problems and improve performance in a project and b) aimed at understanding others or ourselves (Λιντζέρης, 2007; Καγιαβή, 2016).

It constitutes a crucial process in the problem-solving procedure as long as it reframes initial reasoning and assumptions and encourages the adoption of a critical viewing of our previous distorted beliefs (Fisher, 2003). Dissatisfaction and problems result from our dysfunctions and difficulty adapting to the new conditions we discovered while forming our perceptions.

4.2. Aporia and Disorienting Dilemma. Do they have the same meaning?

According to Aristotle (Mantzanaris, 2018; Aristotle et al., I, 8-9, 17b, 8-11), dialectic constitutes a crucial condition of arguments, which form the interrogative determinants of aporia, posing the suitable aporia each time according to the searching proposition that is put forward.

Aristotle notes that "**a dialectical proposition is a question which accords with the opinion held by everyone or by the majority or by the wise**" (Mantzanaris, 2018; Aristotle, Topics: A 10, 104a, 8-9).

Aristotle used the term aporia to refer to a state of puzzlement, confusion, or difficulty that arises during philosophical inquiry. An aporia is a point in an argument or discussion where it seems that there is a logical impasse or contradiction, and it is often used as a starting point for deeper philosophical exploration. Aristotle believed that encountering aporia was an essential part of the philosophical process. Aporia indicates a gap in our understanding or reasoning, which could lead to further investigation and refining of our ideas. Aristotle's approach to dealing with aporia involved a dialectical method of inquiry, where opposing viewpoints or contradictions were carefully examined to reach a more comprehensive and refined understanding of the subject.

In summary, aporia, as Aristotle discussed, refers to a state of intellectual perplexity or difficulty encountered during philosophical inquiry, and it is seen as a catalyst for further philosophical exploration and clarification.

According to Mezirow, the **disorienting dilemma (the Aristotelian aporia, in other words**) can result from an enlightening conversation or a work of art while contacting a different culture of thought and attitude. In this way, because of a crisis experienced during our life (Mezirow, 1978; Malkki, 2012), those conditions are formed with our initial assumptions and reshape our opinions towards a different and unprecedented direction of our life (Laros, 2017; Tayrol, 2000).

The intellectual models that can ram are those in which we can find "deeply ingrained assumptions, generalizations, or even pictures and images that influence how we understand the world and how we take action" (Senge, 1990, p. 8).

To conclude, Aporia (according to Aristotle) and Disorienting dilemma (according to Mezirow) have almost the same meaning. An aporia is a point in an argument where it seems that there is a logical impasse, and it is often used as a starting point for deeper philosophical exploration. Aporia could lead to further investigation and refining of our ideas. A disorienting dilemma is a crisis that someone faces and can provoke a reshaping of ideas, thoughts, and emotions.

4.3. Dialogue is common for both thinkers

Dialogue is undoubtedly commonplace for both thinkers. Mezirow proposes a **reflective course** toward the truth; we transform our previous convictions. Freire's impact on the development of Mezirow's set of thoughts is encouraging critical consciousness by analyzing questions and assuming social action based on dialogue and critical consciousness (Freire, 1973; Taylor, 1998; Harris et al., 2008; Mantzanatis, 2018).

In Greek philosophy, the Socratic **τι εστιν** and the Aristotelian **τι ον είναι** are brought back in this survey of consciousness, highlighting the social dimension of the question. In these terms, as was the Aristotelian proposition, dialogue is included as a channel of prolific reassessment of our convictions. In his Rhetoric, Aristotle discusses dialogue as a tool for persuasion. He explores how different types of speeches and rhetorical techniques can sway audiences by appealing to their emotions, sense of reason, or ethical values. He saw value in a conversational approach to persuasion.

Both thinkers highlight dialogue as a tool for deepening understanding. Aristotle's dialectic approach and Mezirow's transformative discourse aim to refine one's beliefs, moving from unexamined opinions to grounded knowledge. Aristotle's perspective on knowledge involves a structured inquiry through dialectic (or structured dialogue), rhetoric, and ethical relationships, which he saw as essential for personal and communal growth. Aristotle and Mezirow converge on the belief that dialogue is not merely an exchange of ideas but a means to foster meaningful growth. For Aristotle, this is a path toward achieving a virtuous, flourishing life within a community, while for Mezirow, it is a pathway to transforming one's worldview. Dialogue, thus, is essential in both their views as it challenges assumptions, builds community, and promotes personal and social development.

4.4. The meaning of experience for both thinkers

Aristotle and Jack Mezirow provided influential frameworks for understanding "experience" in education, albeit in different contexts and eras. Their approaches differ in purpose and method but intersect in recognizing that experience plays a crucial role in personal growth and learning.

According to Aristotle, knowing what is correct or appropriate to do demands prior experience. Experience is the proper way for someone to decide what is right or what is wrong to do. When experience imparts in a person practical wisdom, then Aristotle views it as axiomatic that ethical behavior will result, as 'it is impossible to be practically wise without being good' (Aristotle, 1925, p. 1144) όπως αναφέρεται στο (Pittman, 2011). According to Aristotle, practical wisdom depends on each person's experience.

The learner's experience is the starting point and subject matter for transformative learning (Mezirow, 1995). Mezirow suggested that intense, emotional experiences were fertile grounds for transformative learning. Experience is constructed according to social data and constantly reconstructed due to changes.

To sum up, Aristotle sees experience as a pathway to virtue and practical wisdom built through habituation and observation. In contrast, Mezirow sees it as a catalyst for transformation, achieved through critical reflection and re-examination of beliefs. Both recognize that experience profoundly shapes human growth. However, Aristotle focuses on moral development within a stable framework of virtues, while Mezirow focuses on the capacity of experience to change the individual's worldview and foster autonomy.

4.5. Eudaimonia or transformation?

Mezirow believes that through critical reflection and critical dialogue, man transforms the existing frame of reference and ill-formed and stereotypical perceptions, eliminating the rigidities and burdens of the past. This is the ultimate goal achieved through the process of transformation. In the context of Jack Mezirow's theory of transformative learning, transformation is a process of critical reflection that leads to profound changes in one's worldview, assumptions, and understanding of oneself.

Transformation is not about adhering to a set of virtues but about questioning and, if necessary, changing the beliefs that define how one sees the world.

At this point, Aristotle differentiates himself and believes that man does not transform. His highest goal is the conquest of eudaimonia, which he learns to seek throughout his life once he has been taught ethics.

Aristotle states that if we are happy, we owe it to ourselves to live virtuously. A virtuous life is not a means of achieving an aspiration but of realizing this pursuit. Blessing presupposes excellence, the greater possible realization of human potential, such as friendship, wisdom, social life, and knowledge. (Spiridaki, 2019).

Eudaimonia is a central concept in Aristotle's ethical philosophy. It is often translated as "happiness" or "flourishing," but it represents a deeper and more nuanced understanding of well-being and the good life. According to Aristotle, eudaimonia is the ultimate goal of human life and the highest good.

Aristotle believed that eudaimonia is achieved by pursuing virtue and developing moral and intellectual qualities. He argued that humans have a unique function: to use rationality to live a life following reason and fulfill their potential. Therefore, eudaimonia involves living a life of virtue and excellence, where a person is in harmony with their true nature and actively engages in the rational and virtuous activities that make them human.

Aristotle identified virtues such as courage, wisdom, justice, and temperance, which he believed were essential for achieving eudaimonia. Virtuous actions and behaviors should result from a balanced and harmonious life, avoiding extremes and finding the "golden mean" between excess and deficiency in one's actions. It is important to note that Aristotle's concept of eudaimonia is not a simple hedonistic pursuit of pleasure or the absence of pain; it is a more profound and enduring state of well-being connected to living a life of moral and intellectual excellence. Eudaimonia is a lifelong endeavor involving personal growth and realizing one's potential as a human being.

Aristotle's ideas about eudaimonia have profoundly influenced Western ethical and philosophical thought and continue to be studied and discussed in ethics, virtue ethics, and moral philosophy.

Eudaimonia, often translated as "happiness" or "flourishing," is a central concept in Aristotle's ethical philosophy. In his works, Aristotle, a Greek philosopher who lived in the 4th century BCE, explored the nature of human well-being and how it relates to ethical virtue, particularly in his Nicomachean Ethics.

Here are some critical points about Aristotle's concept of eudaimonia:

1. Ultimate Goal: Aristotle argues that the ultimate goal of human life is to achieve eudaimonia. It is the highest good and the end toward which all human actions and choices are directed. Eudaimonia is the state of living well and flourishing as a human being.

2. Virtue Ethics: Aristotle's ethics are often called virtue ethics. He believes that eudaimonia is closely tied to the cultivation of moral virtues, such as courage, justice, wisdom, and temperance. Virtues are character traits or dispositions enabling individuals to live morally and intellectually virtuous lives.

3. Rationality: Central to Aristotle's view is that humans are rational animals, and our rationality distinguishes us from other living beings. Eudaimonia is closely related to the exercise of reason and intellectual virtues. According to Aristotle, living following reason is an essential part of flourishing.

4. Balance and Moderation: Aristotle emphasizes the importance of finding a balance or means between extremes. For example, courage is the meaning between recklessness and cowardice, and generosity is between extravagance and stinginess. Virtuous behavior involves finding the right balance in various aspects of life.

5. External Goods: While Aristotle acknowledges the importance of external goods like wealth, health, and social status, he argues that these are not sufficient on their own to attain eudaimonia. True well-being comes from using these external goods to promote human flourishing.

6. Self-Realization: Eudaimonia involves self-realization and fulfilling one's potential as a human being. This includes the development of intellectual, moral, and social capacities.

7. Community and Friendship: Aristotle also emphasizes the importance of human relationships and community. He believes that eudaimonia is not attainable in isolation but is closely connected to the bonds of friendship and participation in a well-ordered community.

In summary, Aristotle's concept of eudaimonia is the idea of living a fulfilled and flourishing life intimately connected to developing moral and intellectual virtues, exercising reason, and pursuing a balanced and virtuous existence. It is the ultimate goal of human life and is achieved through a life well-lived by these principles.

Ultimately, eudaimonia is about actualizing potential within a stable moral framework, while Mezirow's transformation theory emphasizes redefining oneself through critically examining beliefs and assumptions. Both contribute to a fulfilling life, but the path one chooses may depend on whether one prioritizes continuous, virtue-based growth or transformative, self-directed change.

FIFTH CHAPTER

About ethics and adult educators

According to a broad definition, an adult educator is considered to be a person who is engaged in any instructive, advisory, administrative/organizational activity and a program development concerning adult education (Jarvis & Wilson, 1999:10, 272; Darkenwald & Merriam, 1982, pp. 16-17; Knox, 1985, p. 183).

However, adhering to Aristotle and Mezirow, it is equally crucial to characterize and elucidate these abilities as a component of a lifetime ethical investigation. In the absence of such an assumption, moral education exhausts itself in the meandering from error to error, moral life is inevitably reduced to the experience of anxiety and restlessness, moral conscience appears as ambiguous and insincere, and individual autonomy is deprived of all content and determinations (Karavakou, 2018).

Caffarella (1988) analyzes ethical quandaries using Brockett's approach, arguing that they are an unavoidable aspect of teaching adults. Individuals' teaching methods, subject matter, and interactions with pupils are influenced by their personal value system, which is the first dimension. The way teachers treat students equally, regardless of their race, gender, ethnic origin, or creed, and whether they think adults can learn irrespective of age, social class, or prior learning experiences are all influenced by their value systems. When teachers' values regarding appropriate behavior in a learning environment diverge from those of their students, they may find themselves in a difficult ethical position. For instance, educators with a humanistic perspective on people typically see their work as that of a facilitator, who views themselves as catalysts in the learning process and has a tendency to be more student-directed in their instruction. Some learners, however, can object to this method and think that the instructor will only employ lectures and exams rather than helping them become self-directed learners (Caffarella, 1988). When presented with this choice, the educator must determine whether to stick to the track that best suits their understanding of human nature or to go off course.

Regarding the component, which involves considering numerous duties, Caffarella notes that teaching people is rarely a full-time job. Ethical quandaries may arise when other obligations clash with teaching or are given precedence over teaching—people whose primary function is not teaching (Susan, 1991).

According to Aristotle, the orator can cultivate a way of thinking and moral self-improvement in his audience. According to Mezirow, the adult educator can transform his adult learners through critical consciousness. The orator's ethos is the most significant evidence to convince listeners (Iliou, 1984).

According to Aristotle, ethics did not aim at knowledge but character formation (. H.N. 1094b 19 - 1095a 6) (Δραγώνα-Μονάχου, 2015). Ethics had a deeper purpose than the simple transmission of knowledge. It is intended to sculpt and mold people's character based on pure virtues and values. It is being understood that, and in agreement with the two great thinkers, the goal of the adult educator is not the simple transfer of knowledge but the development of character by ethical principles.

5.1. Aristotle's virtue ethics inform adult educator ethics

Aristotle is known to have been Alexander the Great's teacher. Alexander said the well-known phrase, "To my father, I owe life, but to my teacher, I ought to live!" Alexander's respect for human dignity resulted from his studies with Aristotle.

The educator's task is to ensure that trainees learn to rule as free people and that their education will lead them to make the right decisions. Humans have no consensus over what should be taught; thus, we focus on virtue and lead them to the most excellent possible life.

It also needs to be clarified if education focuses primarily on intellectual or moral excellence. The current procedure is confusing; no one knows our actions' guiding principles. Some questions arise, such as: Should virtue be pursued in life, or should the use of higher knowledge be the foundation of our instruction? All viewpoints have been discussed. Once more, regarding the methods available, there is agreement: various persons, beginning with multiple concepts regarding the nature of virtue, inevitably diverge over its application. (Jerold, 1973)

Moreover, the importance of adult educator character, as Mezirow says, and orator character, as Aristotle says, is enormous because the advisory speech of both leads people or adult learners to acquire the city's happiness or to a deep knowledge of themselves. Mezirow also recognized that teachers provided significant support for the learning experience, if not pre-requisite (Pittman, 2011). According to Aristotle, the orator can cultivate a way of thinking and moral self-improvement in his audience. According to Mezirow, the adult educator can transform his adult learners through critical consciousness. The orator's ethos is the most significant evidence to convince listeners (Iliou, 1984).

While Aristotle did not specifically address adult education, his ethical framework offers valuable insights:

- Practical Wisdom: Practical wisdom (phronesis) is paramount in adult education. As Aristotle defines it, this virtue is the art of making the right choice for the right reason, in the right way, and in every situation. It extends the Academy's 'reason' to teach ethics (Aristotle, 1925, p. 1142). Aristotle's belief that experience is gained through time leads to the conclusion that mature individuals are more likely to possess phronesis than younger ones. This combination of age and accessibility makes phronesis a perfect pedagogical framework for adult education. Breier and Ralphs (2009) represent the most recent—and possibly the only—effort to empirically define and clarify practical wisdom in an adult educational setting (Pitman, 2011), further underscoring the importance of this virtue in adult education.

Practical wisdom is the ability to make the right choice for the right reason, in the right way, in every situation. Aristotle discusses the powers of the soul linked to practical wisdom, focusing on the relationship between moral and intellectual powers to achieve the ultimate goal of practical and theoretical wisdom. A person with practical wisdom must link moral virtues to practical reasoning, possessing virtues such as understanding the object of wish, grasping the object of choice, issuing commands well, having the power of understanding, and the power of good sense.

It is not always self-evident that a person can inspire others to do what he/she decides. Aristoteles claims that it is an art of knowing how to treat people so they, too, will agree with your position and will want to follow your orders. Aristotle is often criticized for being 'elitist,' as his standards are attainable by only a few, making human excellence undemocratic. However, Greek paideia aims to develop society's souls, including women and slaves, to the highest level possible. The mark of excellence in practical wisdom is a leader who can build trust and goodwill among citizens rather than assuming superiority.

Aristotle distinguishes between different types of knowledge or wisdom. "Theoretical wisdom" (theoria) pertains to knowledge about abstract and theoretical matters, while "practical wisdom" (phronesis) is concerned with making practical and ethical decisions in everyday life. Phronesis is the virtue that helps individuals determine the morally correct course of action in specific situations.

The ancient Greek philosopher Aristotle significantly contributed to studying rhetoric and oratory. **Orator- according to Aristotle- is the adult educator for us.** In his work "Rhetoric," Aristotle outlined the characteristics and qualities of a compelling orator, so we automatically realize that the characteristics and factors of the orator mentioned by Aristotle are also addressed to the adult educator. According to Aristotle, a skilled orator possesses the following factors:

1. Ethos: Ethos refers to the speaker's character and credibility. Aristotle emphasized that an orator should be perceived as trustworthy, competent, and of good moral character. Establishing credibility with the audience is crucial to persuade them.

2. Logos: Logos refers to using logical reasoning and arguments in persuasive speech. An effective orator should present well-structured and compelling arguments based on evidence and reason. The use of logic helps persuade the audience through rational appeals.

3. Pathos: Pathos relates to the emotional appeal of the speech. Aristotle recognized the power of emotions in persuasion. A skilled orator should be able to evoke the appropriate emotions in the audience to connect with them emotionally.

4. Knowledge: Aristotle believed an orator should deeply understand the subject. This knowledge enhances the speaker's credibility and allows them to make well-informed arguments.

5. Style: Effective orators should master style, including appropriate language, tone, and figurative devices. A well-crafted and engaging style can capture the audience's attention and make the message memorable.

6. Delivery: Aristotle emphasized the importance of effective delivery, which includes factors like voice modulation, gestures, and body language. A confident and engaging delivery can enhance the impact of the speech.

7. Adaptation: A skilled orator should be able to adapt their speech to the specific audience and context. Different situations may require different rhetorical approaches, and an orator should be flexible in their communication style.

8. Memory: In Aristotle's time, orators often had to rely on memory since written texts and teleprompters were unavailable. Developing a solid memory for the content of the speech was considered an essential skill.

Ethics demonstrate a conviction that everyone has access to practical wisdom due to individual experiences. Since "no one is regarded to be a philosopher by nature, humans are thought to have judgment, understanding, and intuitive Teaching ethics beyond the Academy "reason," the powers of judgment, comprehension, and intuition are natural endowments (Aristotle, 1925, p. 1142). Because experience is gained through time, Aristotle concludes that mature individuals are more likely to possess phronesis than younger ones. Age and accessibility combine to make phronesis a perfect pedagogical framework for adult education. In this regard, the most recent—possibly the only—effort to empirically define and clarify practical wisdom in an adult education setting (Pitman, 2011).

It argues that caution cannot be either. As it changes, science is not art but a genuine and reasonable practice of human goods, a virtue (Triantafillidou, 2018).

This involves making sound ethical judgments and decisions, adapting teaching methods to meet learners' needs, and facilitating meaningful learning experiences. *In his Nicomachean Ethics, Aristotle distinguishes between Sophia - the abstract conceptualization of universal truths - and phronesis - acting to improve the quality of life. The latter is based on variable principles, making it a virtue and not an art* (Aristotle, 1925). Phronesis, often translated as "practical wisdom" or "practical reason," is central to Aristotle's ethical and political thought.

Aristotle believed that achieving a virtuous and well-balanced life requires the cultivation of phronesis. It involves the ability to discern the mean between excess and deficiency in one's actions, following the golden mean, a central concept in Aristotle's ethics. Phronesis is developed through experience, practice, and ethical education.

Phronesis is crucial in Aristotle's ethical and political philosophy, helping individuals make sound moral judgments and live virtuous lives.

- **Personal Development:** Adult educators should recognize that education is about acquiring knowledge, **personal growth, and flourishing**. They should support learners in their pursuit of **eudaimonia, promoting self-reflection** and the **development** of **moral character**.

- **Moral Character:** Adult educators should strive to cultivate virtuous qualities in themselves and their learners. By exemplifying virtues like patience, fairness, and integrity, educators can provide moral guidance and be role models for their students.

Aristotle's Rhetoric offers, over time, a diversity of forms of practical discourse from which it springs the character of the orator (Triantari, 2015). The success of practical speech depends on the virtuous character of the orator, who will be distinguished for his excellent knowledge of humans. Therefore, the ability to persuade depends directly on the morality and virtue of the orator. An important role is played by the orator's character so that he can convince his audience. The advisory speech of the orator guides the acquisition of happiness in the city and of the citizens as individuals and citizens (Triantari, 2015).

5.2. Mezirow about ethics and adult educators

The morality of encouraging transformational learning in adult education classes is a concern, meaning that perspectives or habits of mind include values, moral ethics involving conscience, ethical norms, and values (Mezirow, 1978). Education is a social endeavor that brings individuals with varying perspectives and senses of duty together. Accountability is a procedure where there are multiple correct ways to instruct. Additionally, adult education aims to engage in social intervention, frequently leading to societal and personal transformation with unforeseen and irreversible consequences (Merriam & Caffarella, 1999). Thus, nurturing Transformational education "becomes a social and moral activity."

Intervention combined with moral conundrums of right against wrong against incorrect" (p. 371). For example, the mere fact that we, as adult educators, think that encouraging transformative learning is ideal for our students might not accurately represent the aspirations and goals of the students themselves or even the establishment where we work as teachers.

This moral conundrum poses several issues that require more discussion, like: Do we have the correct way to push students and learners to change and transform? How morally right is it to establish circumstances that will place them in such emotionally taxing encounters in the classroom? As adult educators, are we equipped to deal with the accountability connected to such modification? These kinds of inquiries have yet to be examined and require further investigation depth as subjects for conversation in the classroom, as well as potential (Taylor, 2000).

We present the approach of Mezirow, referring to some ethical principles in adult education:

Respect for Learners: Adult educators should respect learners' autonomy and dignity. They should create a safe and inclusive learning environment that encourages open dialogue, critical reflection, and exploration of diverse viewpoints.

Empowerment and Empathy: Adult educators should strive to empower learners by facilitating their growth and development. They should be empathetic, understanding the learners' unique backgrounds and experiences and supporting them in their transformative journey.

Ethical Responsibility: Adult educators promote ethical reasoning and social justice. They should encourage learners to critically examine their values, assumptions, and biases, fostering an ethical and socially conscious mindset.

We continue with the approach of Mezirow (1991), referring to what is **not** ethical for an adult educator to do:

- Deliberately **accelerate** transformative learning without ensuring the learner fully understands that such transformation can occur.

- **Facilitates** a transformation of thinking when its consequences may involve risky actions.

- **Deciding** which of the learner's beliefs should be questioned or challenged.

- **He presents his theory,** which may significantly influence the trainee.

- **He refuses to help a trainee** take action because his personal beliefs conflict with the trainee's.

- **Makes** educational interventions when mental distortions seem to hinder the trainee's progress if the adult educator is not trained as a psychotherapist. (Mezirow, 1991, οπ. Μτφρ. Koulaouzidis, 2022).

The learner is expected to encounter difficulties when he is encouraged to think critically and reflect on some issues through a different prism, putting himself in the transformation process. This does not mean that emancipatory education has no place in this process. However, the adult educator must allow him to act if he feels ready. The ultimate goal is for the adult educator to realize the causes of their problems and, by extension, to improve the quality of their decisions. Helping learners to think critically about their formed assumptions and to be able to challenge and reformulate them with the support and guidance of adult educators is an acceptable act. It falls under the ethical conduct of the adult educator. It is unacceptable for adult educators to attempt to impose their opinions on the trainees, forcing them to adopt them. However, if the instructor disagrees with any procedure emerging from the reflective dialogue, he may withdraw from the educational intervention, explaining the reasons.

Conclusions

Since Jack Mezirow initially proposed the idea of transformative learning, it has become a crucial and increasingly important role in education. The value of autonomy is widely acknowledged because it is (a) the distinguishing characteristic of the post-enlightenment age, personal introspection, and (b) the fundamental component of education.

Adopting the Aristotelian concept of phronesis would be highly beneficial to modern moral teaching and Mezirow's transformative learning. According to Aristotle and Mezirow, moral learning encompasses the practice of morality. Acquiring morality does not mean immediately understanding moral and rational requirements. This is a success of the entire maieutic process, which involves our active involvement (Karavakou, 2018).

The educator is an expert, an authoritarian, a transmitter of knowledge who directs the learning process, while the learner's role is to cultivate intellect, criticism, and abstract thought and to constantly seek knowledge resulting from cultural tradition (Gioti, 2010).

It is impossible to claim that Mezirow follows Aristotle or that Aristotle poses psychological interrogative propositions. Comparing the two thinkers was not random, as it constituted a crucial question regarding discovering truth while examining reflection in adult education. Dilemma or aporia, however, constitutes a mutual position and forms the terms of an existential quest. s.

Jack Mezirow and Aristotle have contributed to ethical matters in their respective fields. While Mezirow is known for his work in transformative learning theory, Aristotle is renowned for his contributions to virtue ethics.

Mezirow's transformative learning theory emphasizes the ethical responsibilities of adult educators, such as respecting learners, empowering them, and fostering ethical reasoning.

Aristotle's virtue ethics highlights the importance of moral character, practical wisdom, and personal development in the role of adult educators.

- **<u>Combining these perspectives can guide adult educators in creating transformative and ethically grounded learning experiences.</u>**

- **<u>Hence, the examination of the two thinkers leads to the production of new questions within the academic dialogue and during the investigation of our course as human beings.</u>**

A transformative learning experience can occur when educators and students are receptive to communicating with one another in safe and open group environments, taking part in demanding experiential activities and exploring learning beyond the rational to include the extrarational. Adult educators must be mindful of one crucial caution: We are entering a field that we are only now starting to comprehend and has many unknowns. More research is also needed because many adult educators must gain the necessary skills to promote transformative learning. "The field naively and unwittingly encourages adult educators to practice incompetently about facilitating transformative learning," it might be claimed with clarity (Robertson, 1996, p. 50).

It is evident that ethics play a crucial role in adult education, but educators must become more sensitive to and conscious of ethical issues. The following suggestions are made by Brockett (1990) to encourage moral behavior in adult education. Personal value systems provide the foundation for comprehending practice ethics, but they must be stated. Clarifying personal convictions can be facilitated by putting one's philosophy of adult education in writing and thinking about it. Setting aside time for introspection on moral matters, individually and in groups, is crucial for identifying moral conundrums and resolving disputes before they occur in other professions' methods of operation. Understanding how different professions handle moral conundrums might help one understand the In the discussion on ethics in adult education, it appears that the path of ethics has difficult points that need special attention from those who deal with the educational process. It is an essential component and should be included in the teaching method of all adult learners. According to Aristotle, ethics is taught, and according to Mezirow, the transformation of adults must occur unhurriedly and spontaneously, seeking the utmost respect for their personality and way of thinking.

Bibliography

Aristotle Topics. in D. W. Ross ed., Aristotelis Topica et Sophistici Elenchi. Oxford: Clarendon Press 1958.

Aristotle. (1925). Ethical Nicomachea (W. D. Ross, Trans.). London: Oxford University Press.

Aristotle. Nicomachea Ethics. Translated by W.D. Ross and revised by J.O. Urmson. In The Complete Works of Aristotle, edited by Jonathan Barnes. Vol. 2 of the Bollingen series, 1729-1867. Princeton: Princeton University Press, 1984.

Breier, M. and Ralphs, A. (2009). In search of phronesis: Recognizing practical wisdom in the Recognition (Assessment) of Prior Learning, *British Journal of Sociology of Education*, 30(4), 479–93.

Brockett, R. G. (1990). Adult Education: Are We Doing It Ethically? *Journal of adult Education* 19, no. 1 (Fall 1990): 5-12. (EJ 420 855)

Caffarella, R. S. "Ethical Dilemmas in the Teaching of Adults." In ETHICAL ISSUES IN ADULT EDUCATION, edited by R. G. Brockett. New York: Teachers College Press, 1988.

Carlson, R. A. (1988). A code of ethics for adult educators? In R. G. Brockett (Ed.), Ethical issues in adult education (pp. 162–177). New York: Teachers College Press, Columbia University.

Fortaliza, F.C. (2007). Paulo Freire: In His Views On Education. Kinaadman An Interdisciplinary Research Journal, 18 (2),1-7.

Gilman, F. C. (2005). Ethics codes and codes of conduct as tools for promoting an ethical and professional public service: Comparative Successes and Lessons. Prepared for the PREM, the World Bank, Washington, DC. Retrieved February 6, 2018, from https://www.oecd.org/mena/governance/35521418.pdf.

Gioti, L (2010). Adult Education Philosophies Guiding Educational Theory and Practice: The Case of Greek Primary Education Teacher Counselors, The International Journal Learning, Vol 17, Number 2.

Γκότσης, Ι., Τάσσης, Β. (2018), ΑΡΙΣΤΟΤΕΛΟΥΣ, Ηθικά Νικομάχεια. file:///C:/Users/tthom/OneDrive/Desktop/MEZIROW-ARISTOTLE/% _2018-9.pdf.

Gordon, W. (2001). Ethical Issues and Codes of Ethics: Views of Adult Education Practitioners in Canada and the United States. *Adult Education Quarterly,* Vol. 51, No. 3

Δραγώνα-Μονάχου Μ. (2015). Ηθική και βιοηθική. *Επιστήμη και Κοινωνία: Επιθεώρηση Πολιτικής και Ηθικής Θεωρίας,* 8, 1–26. https://doi.org/10.12681/sas.715.

Fisher, C. (2003). Demystifying critical reflection: Defining criteria for assessment. Higher Education Research & Development, 22(3), 313–325.

Freire, P. (1973). Education for critical consciousness. New York: Continuum.

Harris S., Lowery-Moore H., Farrow V. (2008). Extending Transfer of Learning Theory to Transformative Learning Theory: A Model for Promoting Teacher Leadership. Theory Into Practice, 47(4), 318–326.

Jarvis, P. & Wilson, A.L. (1999). International Dictionary of Adult and Continuing Education, London: Kogan Page. Ethics in the Teaching Profession: A Practical Approach to Teachers' Professionalism. *International Journal of Social Sciences and Educational Studies* 10(3), June 2023, DOI:10.23918/ijsses.v10i3p82.

Jerold, W. (1973). Toward a Working Philosophy of Adult Education. Publications in Continuing Education, Syracuse, University, Syracuse, N.Y.

Iliou, H. (1984). Η ρητορική του Αριστοτέλη. Αθήνα: ΚΕΔΡΟΣ.

Καγιαβή, Μ. (2016), Η πολυδιάστατη μάθηση ως παράγοντας μετασχηματισμού στους ενήλικες (Διδακτορική διατριβή). Ελληνικό Ανοικτό Πανεπιστήμιο, Πάτρα.

Kapur. R (2006) Transformative Learning – Theories and Practices

Karavakou, V. (2018). Phronesis and Transformative Learning: A Joint Challenge for Moral Philosophy and Educational Theory, Philosophy Study, August 2018, Vol. 8, No. 8, 383-394, doi: 10.17265/2159-5313/2018.08.005.

Kadlubeková, D. (2016). Základy andragogickej etiky. Nitra: UKF Pedagogická fakulta.

Κόκκος, Α. (2010). Κριτικός Στοχασμός : Ένα κρίσιμο Ζήτημα. Στο Δ. Βεργίδης, Α. Κόκκος (Επιμ.), «Εκπαίδευση Ενηλίκων : διεθνείς προσεγγίσεις και ελληνικές διαδρομές», (σσ. 65 – 93). Αθήνα : Μεταίχμιο.

Κουλαουζίδης, Γ. (2008). Μετασχηματίζουσα μάθηση: μια μαθησιακή θεωρία για την εκπαίδευση ενηλίκων. Παιδαγωγική Επιθεώρηση, τεύχος 46/2008, σελ. 21-32.

Κουλαουζίδης, Γ. (2010). Οι αρχές της εκπαίδευσης ενηλίκων. Πάτρα: ΕΑΠ.

Laros, A. (2017). Disorienting Dilemmas as a Catalyst for Transformative Learning. In A. Laros, T. Fuhr, W.E. Taylor (Eds.), Transformative Learning Meets Bildung. International Issues in Adult Education (pp85-95). Rotterdam: Sense Publisher.

Lesky, A. (1972). Ιστορία της Αρχαίας Ελληνικής Λογοτεχνίας. Αθήνα: Ελληνικό Ίδρυμα Εξυπηρέτησης Πανεπιστημίων.

Λιντζέρης, Π. (2010*). Θεωρία της Μετασχηματίζουσας Μάθησης : Δυνατότητα για μια κριτική και χειραφετική στροφή στην πρακτική της Εκπαίδευσης Ενηλίκων*. Στο Δ. Βεργίδης, Α. Κόκκος (Επιμ.), « Εκπαίδευση Ενηλίκων : διεθνείς προσεγγίσεις και ελληνικές διαδρομές», (σσ. 94 – 123). Αθήνα : Μεταίχμιο.

Κόκκος, Α., Λιοναράκης, Π. (1998). *Ανοικτή και εξ αποστάσεως εκπαίδευση*. ΕΑΠ

Λιντζέρης, Π. (2010). *Η σημασία του κριτικού στοχασμού και του ορθολογικού διαλόγου στη θεωρία του Jack Mezirow για τη Μετασχηματίζουσα Μάθηση*. Αθήνα: Επιστημονική Ένωση Εκπαίδευσης Ενηλίκων

Malach, J. (2020). Ethical codes in adult education as subjects of comparative Analysis - In: European Journal for Research on the Education and Learning of Adults 11 (2020) 2, S. 199-217 - URN: urn: nbn: de:0111-pedocs-202831 - DOI: 10.25656/01:20283.

Mantzanaris K. (2018). The dilemma as a prerequisite of truth according to Mezirow and Aristotle, Scientific Educational Journal "educ@tional circle". Volume 6, Issue 2, 2018 © educ@tional circle ISSN: 2241-4576.

Μέγα. http://neoellines.files.wordpress.com/2009/02/mezirow.pdf (τελευταία πρόσβαση 12.11. 2012).

Mezirow, J. (1978). Perspective Transformation. *Adult Education Quarterly* 28 - Transformative Dimensions of Adult Learning. San Fransisco: Jossey Bass, 1991, ---.

Understanding and Promoting Transformative Learning: A Guide for Educators for Adults. San Francisco, Ca.: Jossey-Bass, 1994.

Mezirow, J. Learning as Transformation: Critical Perspectives on a Theory in Progress. San Francisco, Ca.: Jossey-Bass, 2000.

Mezirow, J. (1978). Perspective Transformation, *Sage Journals*, Volume 28, Issue 2, https://doi.org/10.1177/074171367802800202

Mezirow, J. (1990). Πώς ο κριτικός στοχασμός ενεργοποιεί τη Μετασχηματίζουσα Μάθηση. Μτφρ. Ν. Αποστολοπούλου & Γ.

Mezirow, J. (1991). Transformative dimensions of adult learning. San Francisco: Jossey-Bass.

Mezirow, J. (1995). Transformation theory of adult learning. In M. R. Welton (Ed.). In defense of the lifeworld (pp. 39–70). New York: SUNY.

Mezirow, J. & Associates. (2000). Learning as transformation: Critical perspectives on a theory in progress. San Francisco, CA: Jossey-Bass.

Merriam, S. B., & Caffarella, R. S. (1999). Learning in adulthood. San Francisco: Jossey-Bass.

Mälkki, K. (2012). Rethinking disorienting dilemmas within real-life crises: The role of reflection in negotiating emotionally chaotic experiences. Adult Education Quarterly, 62(3), 207–229.

Palazi, P. (2018). Plato and Aristoteles's views on education. University of Western Macedonia

Pitman, T., Broomhall, S., & Majocha, E. (2011). Teaching ethics beyond the Academy: educational tourism, lifelong learning, and phronesis. Studies in the Education of Adults. Voi.43.

Pitman, T, Broomhall, S., Majocha, E. and McEwan, J. (2010). 'Transformative learning in educational tourism'. Paper presented at the Educating for Sustainability. Proceedings of the 19th Annual Teaching Learning Forum. Retrieved from http://otl.curtin.edu.au/tlf/tlf2010/refereed/pitman. html.

Robertson, D. (1997). Transformative learning and transition theory: Toward developing the ability to facilitate insight. Journal on Excellence in College Teaching, 8, 105-125.

Ρωτίδη, Γ. (2015). Διδακτικές οπτικές και κριτικά στοχαστικές διεργασίες διδασκόντων στην τριτοβάθμια εκπαίδευση: ποσοτική και ποιοτική διερεύνηση με βάση την προσέγγιση Tpi (teaching perspectives inventory), την τυπολογία Biglan και το μοντέλο Soft (scholarship of teaching). (Διδακτορική διατριβή). Πανεπιστήμιο Πατρών.

Susan. I. (1991). Ethical Practice in Adult Education. Source: ERIC *Clearinghouse on Adult Career and Vocational Education Columbus* OH. Ethical Practice in Adult Education. ERIC Digest No. 116

Tarek, T. (2023). The philosophy of education in empowering communities - from ancient Greece to educational technology. International Conference, USA, 2023, October

Taylor, E. W. (1998). The theory and practice of transformative learning: A critical review (Information Series No 374). Columbus, Ohio: ERIC Clearinghouse on Adult, Career, and Vocational Education, Center on Education and Training for Employment, Ohio State University.

Triantari, S. (2015). Η ρητορική του Αριστοτέλη στην ηθική διαπαιδαγώγηση του ανθρώπου [διαδικτυακά]. Διαθέσιμο στο: https://www.academia.edu/25510653/%CE%97_

Triantafillidou, D. (2018). *Aristotle's Ethics and its communicational dimensions today*. University of Western Macedonia.

Taylor, E.W. (2000). Fostering Mezirow's transformative learning theory in the adult education classroom: a critical review. CJSAE/RCEEA 14,2, November.

Theodorakopoulou. T. (2018). Lifelong Learning Education of adults immigrants, Athens: Papazisis.

Sork, T. (2001). *American Association for Adult and Continuing Education*

Filosofikilithos. (n.d.). Η Ηθική Φιλοσοφία στον Αριστοτέλη. https://www.filosofikilithos.gr/i-ithiki-filosofia-ston-aristoteli

Wikepedia. (n.d.). *Herakleitos*. https://el.wikipedia.org/wiki/

Wikepedia. (n.d.). *Herakleitos*. https://el.wikipedia.org/wiki/

www.ingramcontent.com/pod-product-compliance
Lightning Source LLC
LaVergne TN
LVHW010507160826
845677LV00012B/2715